UNDER THE SEA

Leon

Hetty

Professor Verne

Brigit

Toosant

Newton

551.46

Watts Books

London • New York • Sydney

In the nineteenth century Jules Verne, the famous author, wrote exciting books about journeys of adventure. Now his namesake, Professor Bartholemew Verne, has invented an amazing machine. In it he can follow the journeys Jules Verne wrote about. With his crew of children, he can explore the wonders of the world and of outer space.

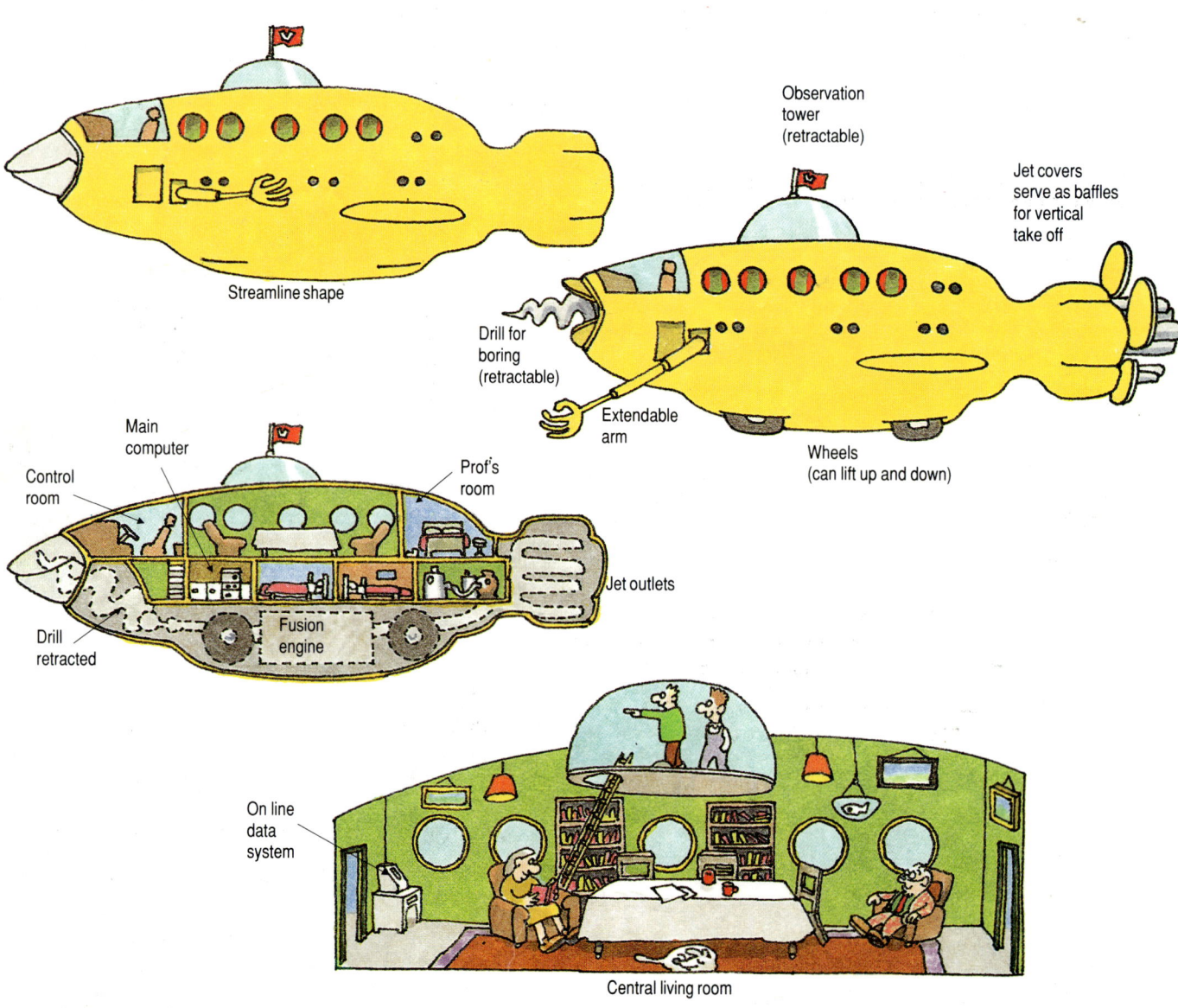

However, as the planet cooled down, the clouds of water vapour turned into rain, and this fell on the Earth. Torrential rain lasted for thousands of years, and millions and millions of litres of water filled up the hollows in the crust of the Earth to create the first seas and oceans.

Sea plants first appeared 3,500 million years ago. These were microscopic blue-green algae which gave off oxygen. After millions of years there were eventually enough algae giving off oxygen to allow animals to live.

Some scientists believe that all the continents were once joined together making a giant continent called Pangaea. This was surrounded by a single ocean called Panthalassa.

About 180 million years ago, Pangaea and Panthalassa began to break. They drifted apart and formed new continents and oceans. These are still drifting today!

Information: **WATER**

Area: **Water covers 360 million sq km of the Earth**
Depth: **Average depth of oceans and seas is 3,554 m**

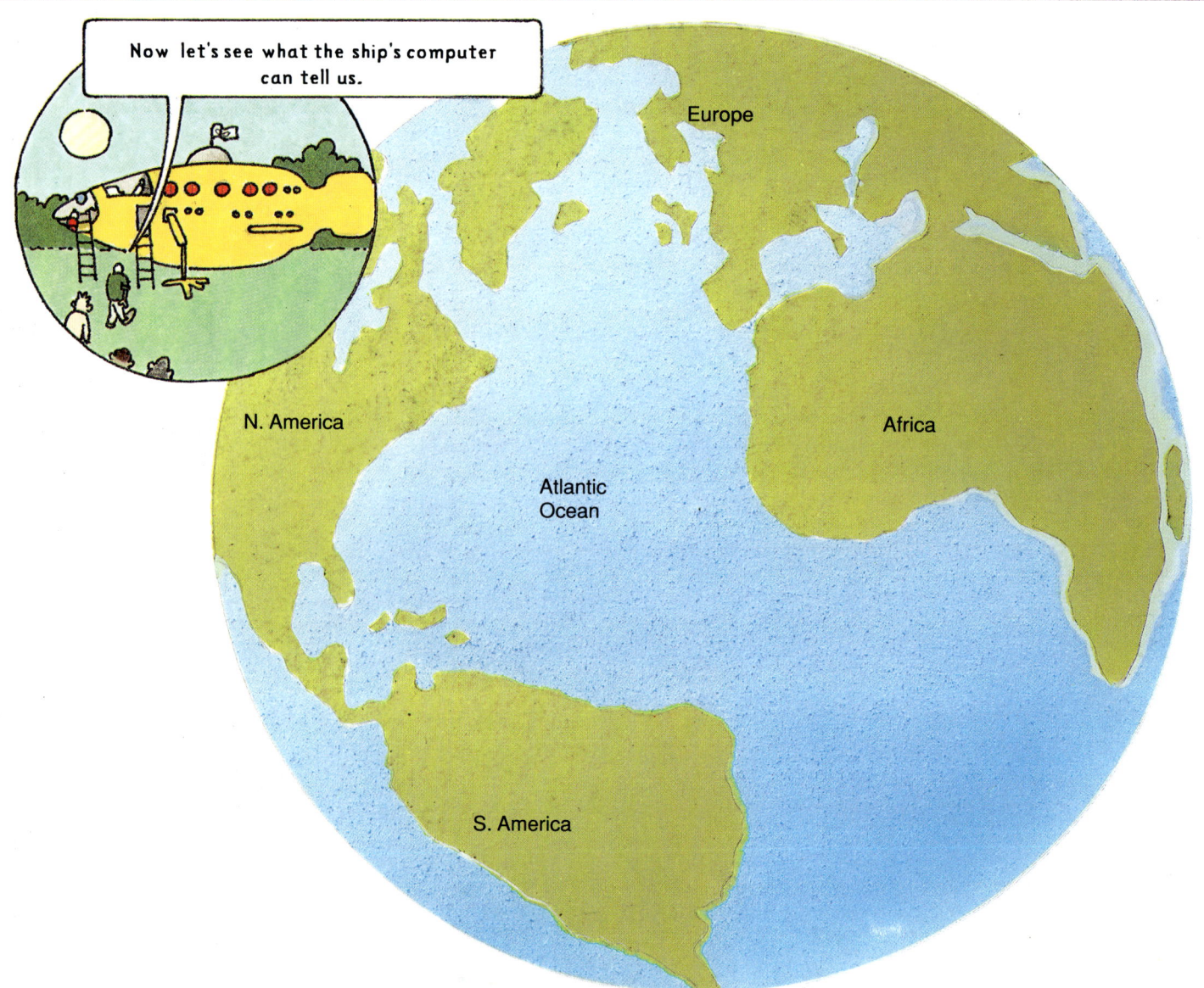

THE PLANET WATER!

Over seventy percent of the Earth's surface is covered by oceans and seas. This is called the *hydrosphere*. 'Hydro' is the Greek word for water. Ninety seven percent of the world's water is salty and is found in the world's oceans and seas.

There are five main oceans: the Pacific, the Atlantic, the Indian, the Arctic and the Southern (sometimes called the Antarctic Ocean). These are all joined together, and water flows between them. There are also many seas that surround the oceans. The largest sea in the world is the South China Sea.

Volume: Oceans contain 1,350 million cubic km
Fresh water contains 35 million cubic km

Weight: 1,320 billion billion tonnes

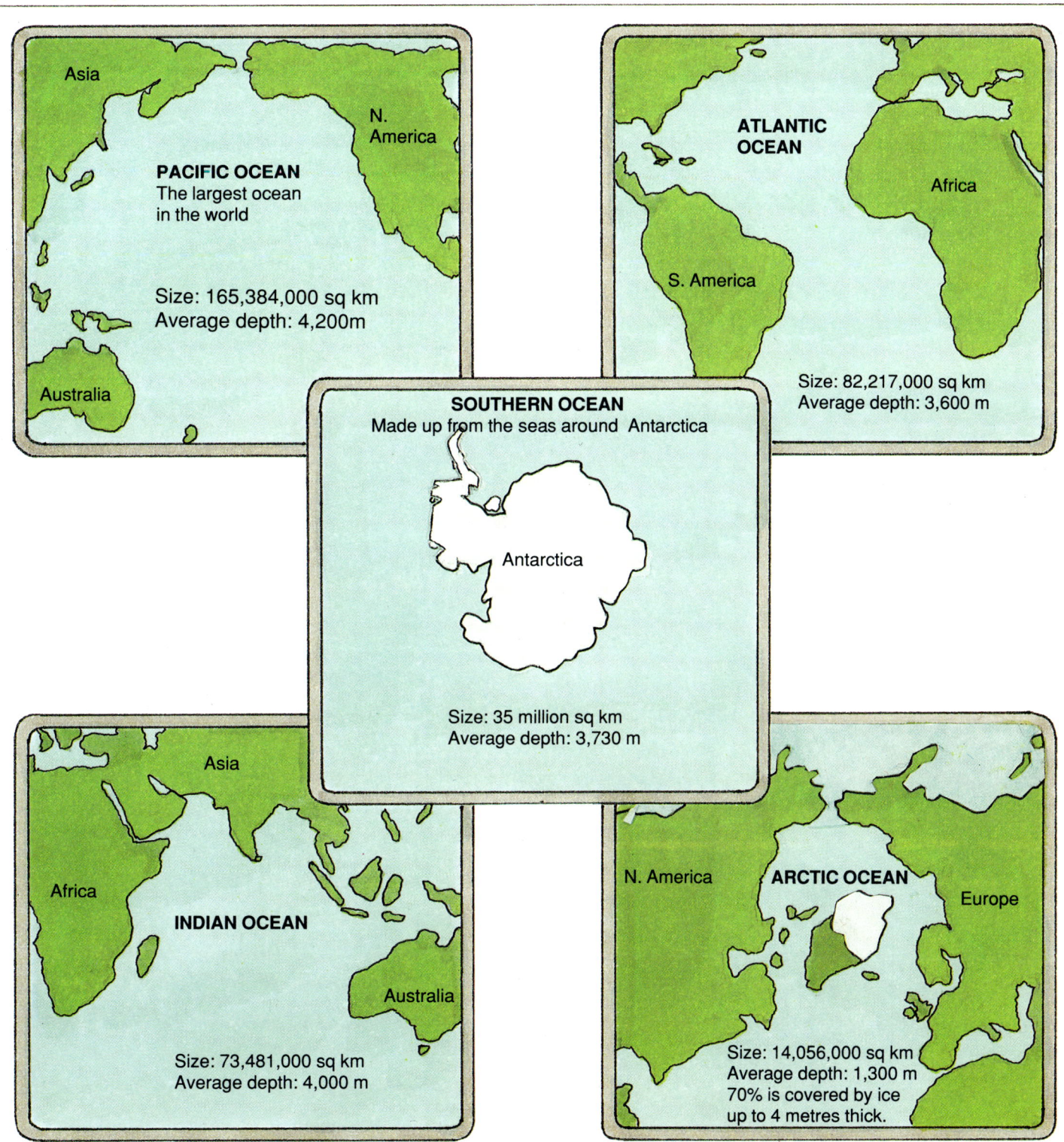

BLAST OFF!

Waves are caused by wind blowing over oceans and seas. They begin as small ripples, but as the wind blows on the surface of the water, it pushes these ripples up, making them into waves. The harder and longer the wind blows, the bigger the waves become. Some waves travel thousands of kilometres before breaking on the shore.

Giant waves are called *tsunamis*. These are caused by earthquakes and under-sea volcanic eruptions. Tsunamis travel at incredible speeds and create sheets of water that can be up to 85 m high. Whole islands and cities have been drowned and destroyed by tsunamis.

COMPU-DATA

Waves do not move water forward! The droplets of water in a wave travel up and down, but end up in the same place. This is why boats bob up and down on a wave.

Destination: **The world's oceans and seas**

Destination: **NORTH SEA CONTINENTAL SHELF**

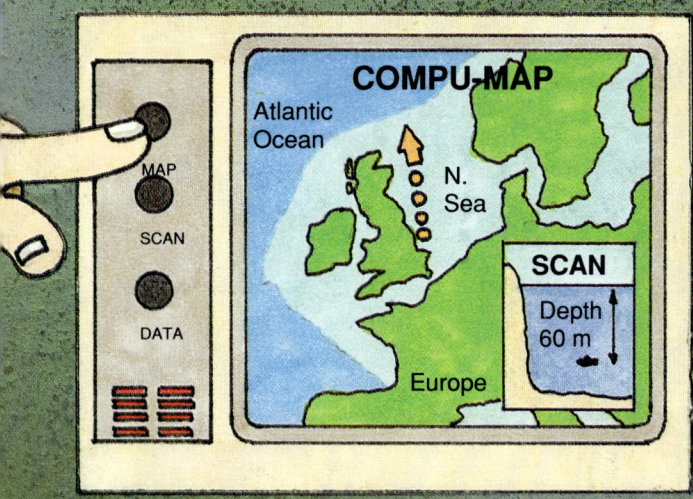

The *continental shelf* is the name given to the shallow area of sea floor that surrounds the continents. It slopes gently to a depth of no more than 200m. It varies in width from 1 to 1,200 km. The shelf's sea floor is generally covered in mud, silt and sand brought down by rivers from the land.

Continental shelves are very important areas. Most of the fish we eat come from the waters above shelves. Most sea creatures live in the top 150 m of the oceans.

The shelf is a rich area for mineral resources. More than a third of the world's oil comes from under the sea bed. Around the world, there are hundreds of off-shore drilling platforms over continental shelves. Metals and other minerals are found on the sea bed of the continental shelf.

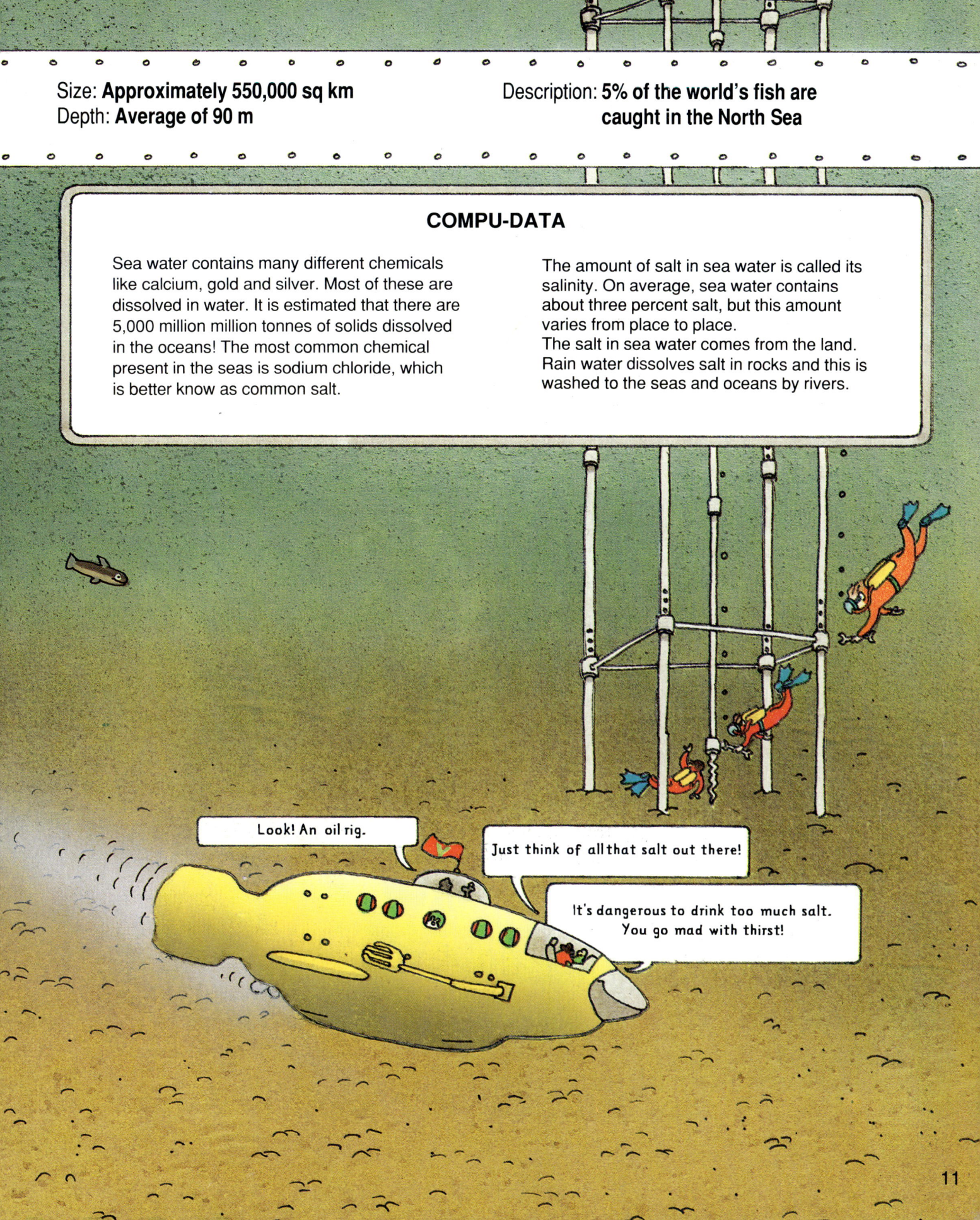

Destination: BAY OF FUNDY, CANADA

The level of the sea is different at certain times of the day. This happens because of the tides.

Tides are caused by gravity. Planets and stars are attracted towards each other by the force of gravity. Without gravity on Earth, we would all be thrown off the planet and be floating in space.

Gravity from the moon tries to pull everything on Earth towards it. Solid objects, such as the ground and mountains, only move a tiny amount. However, water can move and is pulled towards the moon. This movement causes the rise and fall of the sea.

As the Earth spins round, different parts of the seas come closest to the moon. Gravity from the moon causes the water in the seas to bulge towards it. Two bulges are formed, one on each side of the Earth. The bulges in the water reach different oceans as the world spins. The gradual raising and lowering of these bulges is how tides are formed.

Differences in size and shape of the oceans and seas cause tides to vary. The Bay of Fundy has the greatest tides in the world. The total rise and fall can be up to 15 m. In comparison, Tahiti in the Pacific Ocean has virtually no tide change.

Length: **300 km**
Width: **100 km**

Tides: **There are two spring tides and two neap tides every month**

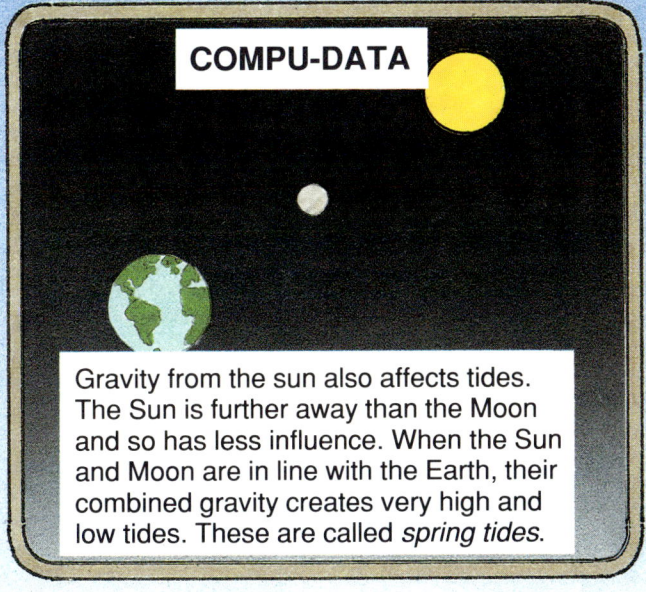

COMPU-DATA

Gravity from the sun also affects tides. The Sun is further away than the Moon and so has less influence. When the Sun and Moon are in line with the Earth, their combined gravity creates very high and low tides. These are called *spring tides*.

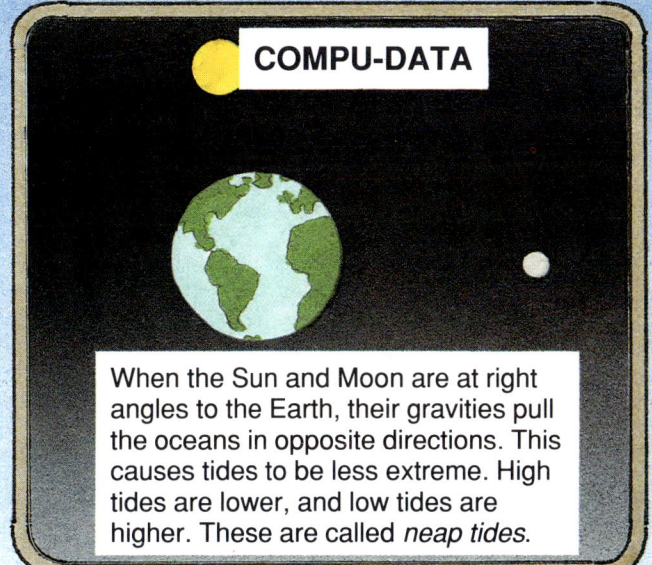

COMPU-DATA

When the Sun and Moon are at right angles to the Earth, their gravities pull the oceans in opposite directions. This causes tides to be less extreme. High tides are lower, and low tides are higher. These are called *neap tides*.

"The water comes up that high."

"We'll get covered if we stay here."

"The tide's coming in!"

13

Destination: **THE GULF STREAM**

There are 1,370 million cubic km of water in the oceans. It is always moving, and this is caused by wind, waves, tides and currents.

The Gulf Stream is one of the world's main currents. It starts along the coasts of central and north-east America and travels across the Atlantic towards Europe. It is a warm surface current.

Surface currents are caused by the wind blowing on the ocean for a long time. Winds push the water along in huge bands. The direction the currents take does not follow the exact course of the wind. The Earth spins, and this causes the currents to change direction. Currents north of the equator curve to the right, and those south of the equator to the left.

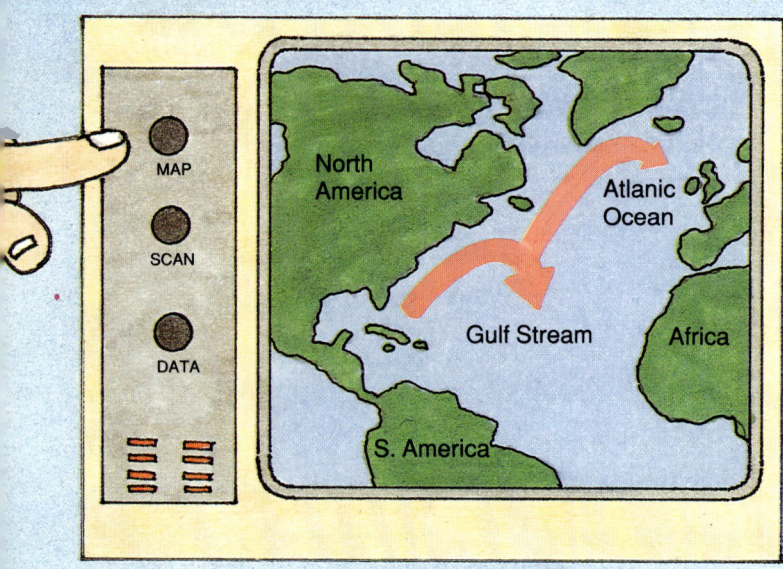

Description: **Warm water current**
Width: **600 km**

Depth: **Up to 60 m**
Speed: **Up to 220 km per day**

There are also deep ocean currents caused by the movement of cold water from the polar regions. When these meet warm currents from the equator, vast spiral currents are created. These are called *gyres*, and occur in all the world's oceans.

COMPU-DATA

Ocean currents also affect the world's climate. Warm currents move away from the equator, warming up places nearer the polar regions. Similarly, the cold currents from the poles cool down hotter regions as they travel towards the equator. Winds blowing over these currents are warmed or cooled by the temperature of the water. This affects the temperature of the land.

Destination: **ATLANTIC OCEAN**

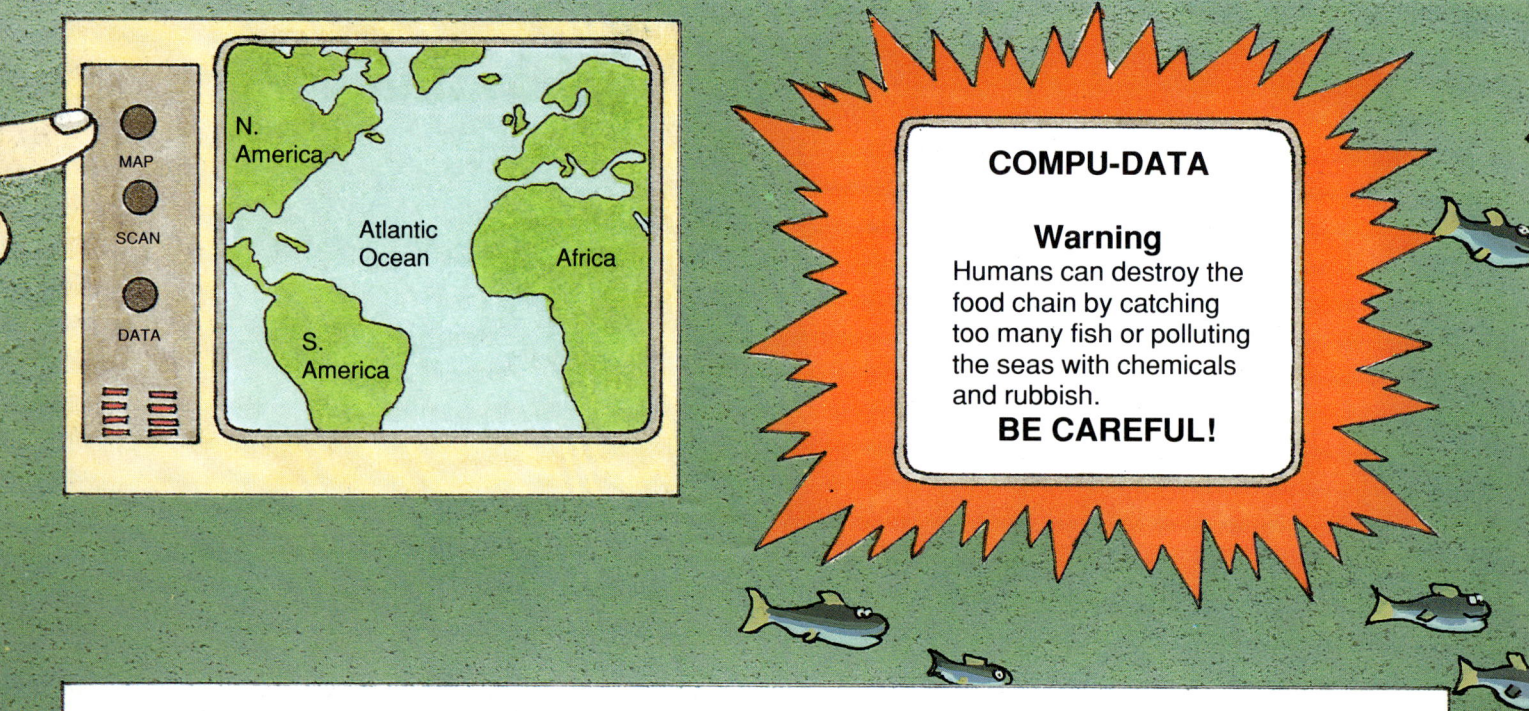

COMPU-DATA

Warning
Humans can destroy the food chain by catching too many fish or polluting the seas with chemicals and rubbish.
BE CAREFUL!

The oceans are home to thousands of different species of creatures. These are divided into three types: *plankton*, *nekton* and *benthos*.

Plankton are microscopic plants and animals that drift where the sea currents take them. The word 'plankton' actually means wanderer.
Nekton are all the free-swimming creatures of the oceans. These include most fishes, whales, seals, squid and reptiles like turtles and sea snakes.
Benthos are the creatures that live on or near the sea bed. These include lobsters, crabs and also the creatures that look like plants, such as sea cucumbers, sponges and anemones.

Some fish are also part of the benthos group.

All sea creatures depend on each other for food. *Phytoplankton* are microscopic plants which are eaten by microscopic animals called *zooplankton*. These are then eaten by fish like herring and sardines. These in turn are eaten by bigger fish such as cod, sharks and tuna.

The droppings from these fish and also bits of dead animals and plants sink to the sea bed, and some of these are eaten by the benthos. Other bits are broken down and become food for the photoplankton. This is called the *food cycle* or the *food chain*.

Fishing: **The Atlantic contains 6 of the world's 14 major fishing grounds**

Major catches: **Herring, Hake, Tuna, Crustaceans**

It's horrible!

What is it?

I don't want to be part of the food chain.

COMPU-DATA

Diatom
Goniaulax
Silicoflagellate
Peridinium granii
Ceratium arcticum

Some types of plankton.

Destination: **SOHM ABYSSAL PLAIN** North Atlantic

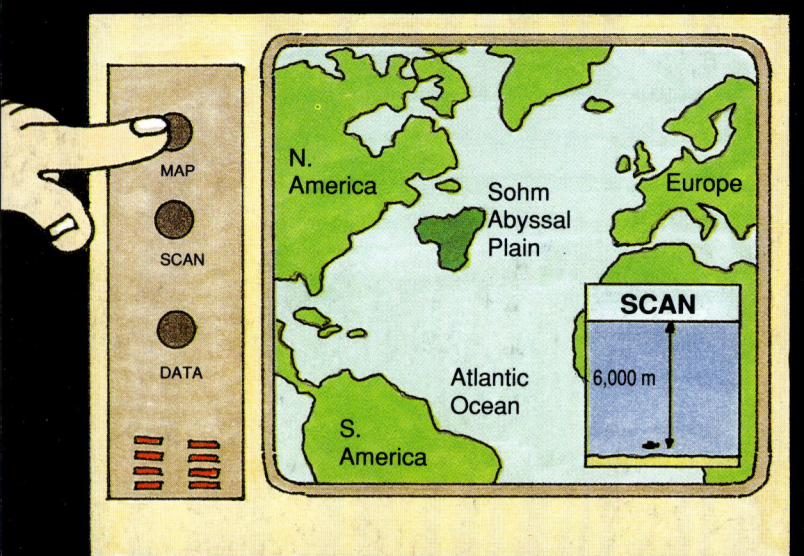

At the edge of the continental shelf, the sea floor slopes steeply away. This area is called the *continental slope*. The sea floor then flattens out into huge empty plains.

Size: **900,000 sq km**
Average depth: **5,000 m**

Temperature: **0°C to 2°C**

These *abyssal plains* cover 75% of the ocean floor and are the flattest places on Earth. They are covered in smooth, fine sediment made up of a mixture of mud and animal and plant remains.

The remains fell there over millions of years. Few creatures live on the abyssal plains. Underwater mountains, ridges and volcanoes occasionally reach up to the surface from the vast empty plain.

Destination: # THE MID-ATLANTIC RIDGE

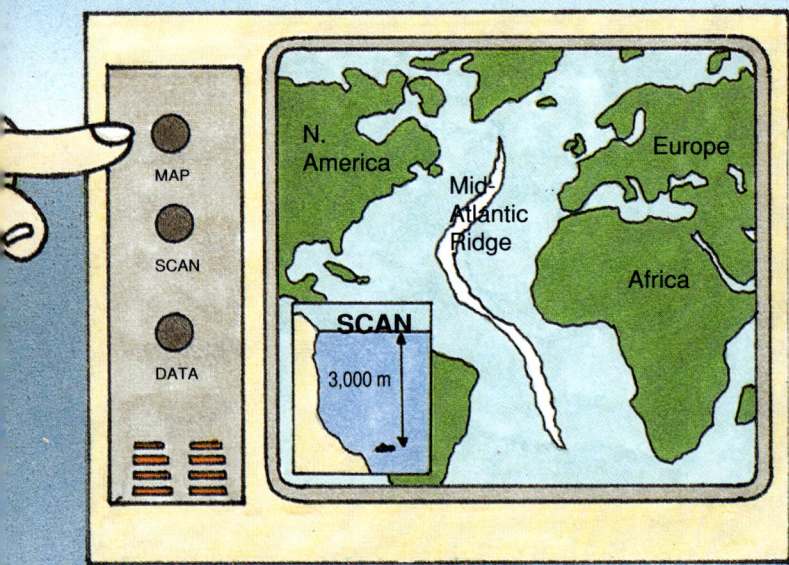

The Mid-Atlantic Ridge is part of the mid-ocean ridge, the largest mountain range in the world. This series of underwater mountains runs through all the world's oceans. It stretches for 65,000 km and rises thousands of metres above the ocean floor. In some places the ridge breaks through the surface of the sea to form islands like the Azores and Iceland.

Mountain ranges are not the only mountains in the sea. Individual underwater volcanoes also exist, and these are called *seamounts*. There are hundreds of these scattered throughout the Pacific.

COMPU-DATA

Mauna Kea

Pacific Ocean

Mount Everest is not the tallest mountain in the world! Mauna Kea, one of the islands of Hawaii in the Pacific Ocean, measures 10,203 m from its submarine base to its summit. Only 4,205 m of Mauna Kea is above the surface of the sea. Mount Everest measures 8,848 m.

Length: **About 11,265 km**
Width: **Up to 1,600 km**

Height: **7,800 m from the greatest depth to the highest peak**

The Mid-Atlantic Ridge is getting bigger every year. This is because of lava being pushed up from under the Earth's crust. As the water cools the lava, it forms into huge sheets of basalt rock.

21

Destination: **THE WEDDELL SEA** Antarctica

The Weddell Sea is part of the Southern Ocean that surrounds the continent of Antarctica. The ocean is very rich in plankton and krill, a small shrimp-like creature.

Krill only measure about 5 cm when fully grown. However, there are such enormous numbers of them that the total weight of krill in the Southern Ocean is estimated to be up to 700 million tonnes.

Krill and plankton provide food for many sea creatures including seals, fish, sea birds and whales. Blue whales may eat up to 4 tonnes of krill every day!

Hundreds of whales migrate to the Southern Ocean during the summer months of November to May. At the end of summer they move north to warmer waters to mate and give birth.

Size: **2,800,000 sq km**
Temperature: **Below -1°C**

Description: **The clearest water of any sea in the world**

Route

SCAN
500 m

S. America
Weddell Sea
Antarctica

COMPU-DATA

There are 82 species of krill. Some krill glow in the dark. Krill are especially rich in vitamin A.

Destination: MARIANAS TRENCH Pacific Ocean

The Marianas Trench is the deepest point on Earth. If a steel ball weighing 1 kg was dropped into the trench, it would take 64 minutes to reach the bottom!

The trench was first explored in 1960 when the bathyscape *Trieste* almost descended to the bottom. A bathyscape is a special type of submarine. It has very strong sides to stop it being crushed by the pressure of the water.

The weight of water creates great pressure. The deeper you go, the more the pressure is. The pressure increases by 1.1 kg per sq cm for every 10 m you go down.

The water pressure in the Marianas Trench is a thousand times greater than at the surface. This pressure would be like ten elephants standing on top of you!

Depth: **About 11,034 m**   Light: **There is no light deeper than 1,000 m**

COMPU-DATA

Deep sea creatures such as the Flash-light fish create their own light because the sea is dark at great depths.

It's so dark!

Let's go back! I'm frightened.

Look! The wreck of a bathyscape. It's been crushed

Destination: **BORA BORA** South Pacific Ocean

Bora Bora is an island formed from an extinct volcano and surrounded by a coral reef. Between the reef and the island is a shallow lagoon. It is one of hundreds of similar coral reef islands in the Pacific.

Tiny animals called *polyps* are responsible for creating coral reefs. These animals have limestone skeletons around their bodies. When they die, their skeletons remain, and new polyps grow on top. Millions of these skeletons pile up on top of each other to create coral reefs.

Coral grows best in water that is warm (17° to 35°C), shallow (no more than 50 m deep), and clean. Because of these conditions, coral can only grow in tropical and sub-tropical seas.

The longest coral reef in the world is the Great Barrier Reef off the coast of Australia. It is over 2,000 km long, and covers an area of 259,000 sq km. It is so big that it can be seen from the moon!

Island: **Length 6.5 km**
Width 4 km

Reef: **Length 14.5 km**
Width 9.5 km

"Coral is very delicate. I hope they're carefull"

COMPU-DATA
There are three different types of coral reef:

Fringing Reefs grow in shallow water close to land.

Barrier Reefs are separated from land by a wide water channel.

Atoll Reefs are ring shaped coral islands formed around sinking volcanic islands.

Destination: **ARCTIC OCEAN**

Volume: **17,000 million cubic km**

Sea water freezes at -2°C. Because of the intense cold in the polar regions, parts of the Arctic and Antarctic Oceans are always frozen. Other areas freeze in winter and thaw in summer.

When sea ice begins to thaw, large chunks of ice break off and are carried away by the current. These chunks are called icebergs.

Icebergs are also created when glaciers melt. Glaciers are rivers of ice, and as they reach the shore, the ice breaks away and falls into the water. This incredibly noisy process is called *calving*. In the Arctic icebergs are created mainly in April, and in the Antarctic mainly in October. Icebergs then drift towards warmer climates where they melt. Some icebergs travel for thousands of kilometres.

Only an eighth of an iceberg is visible. The rest of it is under the water. Because of this, icebergs are very dangerous for ships. On its first voyage in 1912 the *Titanic* was hit by an iceberg and sank. Over 1,500 people died in the freezing waters of the Atlantic Ocean.

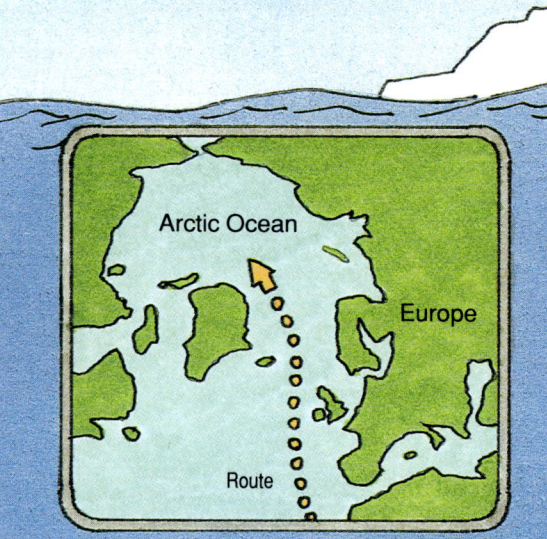

COMPU-DATA

Icebergs come in many shapes and sizes. In 1956 the largest one ever seen was observed in the Southern Ocean. It was 335 km long and 97 km wide, and covered an area of 35,000 sq km which is larger than Belgium! It took 17 years to melt!

Size: **14,056,000 sq km**
Average depth: **1,300 m**

Average thickness of ice: **3 to 3.5 m**
Temperature: **0° to 3°C (32°F to 37° F)**

Now that you've found out all about the oceans, let's see how much you can remember:

1. **What is the tallest mountain in the world?**
   a) Mount Everest
   b) Mount Kea
   c) Marianas Trench

2. **Where is the continental shelf?**
   a) next to the continental duvet
   b) next to the world's coasts
   c) in the kitchen

3. **What is the world's largest ocean?**
   a) the Atlantic
   b) the Pacific
   c) the Indian

4. **What is the deepest point on Earth?**
   a) Manhole Trench
   b) Marianas Trench
   c) Monkey Trench

5. **What causes tides?**
   a) waves
   b) gravity
   c) earthquakes

6. **What does the Greek word 'hydro' mean?**
   a) water
   b) a place to hide
   c) a tall person

7. **What is the chemical symbol for water?**
   a) DNO
   b) H_2O
   c) BBC2

Answers: 1) b 2) b 3) b 4) b 5) b 6) a 7) b

31

INDEX

Abyssal plain 3
Algae 5
Arctic Ocean 28
Atlantic Ocean 7
Australia 26
Azores 20
Barrier reef 27
Bathyscape 24
Bay of Fundy 12
Bora Bora 26
Calving 28
Climate 15
Continental shelf 3, 10
Continental slope 3, 18
Coral 26, 27
Currents 14, 15
Fish 16, 17
Flash-light fish 25
Food cycle 16
Glaciers 28
Gravity 12, 13
Great Barrier Reef 26

Gulf Stream 14
Gyres 15
Hydrosphere 6
Icebergs 28, 29
Indian Ocean 7
Intertidal zone 3
Krill 22
Lava 21
Marianas Trench 24
Mauna Kea 20
Mid-Atlantic Ridge 20, 21
Minerals 10, 11
Mount Everest 20
Neap tides 13
Nekton 16
North Sea 10, 11
Oceans 7
Oil 10
Pacific Ocean 7, 24 – 26
Pangaea 5
Panthalassa 5
Plankton 16, 22

Polyps 26
Quiz 31
Rain 5, 30
Reefs 26, 27
Rivers 11, 30
Salt 11
Sea mounts 20
Sohm Abyssal Plain 18, 19
South China Sea 6
Southern Ocean 7, 22
Spring tides 13
Tides 12
Titanic 28
Tsunamis 8
Volcanoes 4, 26
Water 6
Water cycle 30
Water pressure 24
Waves 8, 9
Weddell Sea 22
Whales 22

This hardback edition first published 1993 by
Watts Books
96 Leonard Street
London
EC2A 4RH

ISBN 0 7496 1296 7

Original edition first published 1992
by Hodder and Stoughton Ltd

© 1992 Steve Skidmore/Lazy Summer Books

The rights of Steve Skidmore to be identified as the author of the text of this work has been asserted by him in accordance with the Copyright, Designs and Patents Act 1988.

All rights reserved. No part of this publication may be reproduced or transmitted in any form or by any means, electronic or mechanical, including photocopy, recording, or any information storage and retrieval system, without permission in writing from the publisher or under licence from the Copyright Licensing Agency Limited. Further details of such licences (for reprographic reproduction) may be obtained from the Copyright Licensing Agency Limited, of 90 Tottenham Court Road, London W1P 9HE.

Printed in Great Britain by Cambus Litho Limited, East Kilbride